HEINEMANN Profiles

Roald Dahl

An Unauthorized Biography

Haydn Middleton

Heinemann Library
Des Plaines, Illinois

Designed by Visual Image
Printed in Hong Kong / China

03 02 01 00 99

10 9 8 7 6 5 4 3 2 1

Library of Congress Cataloging-in-Publication Data
Middleton, Haydn.
    Roald Dahl / Roald Dahl.
      p.   cm. -- (Heinemann profiles)
    Includes bibliographical references and index.
    Summary: A biography of the writer of such popular books as
"Charlie and the Chocolate Factory," "James and the Giant Peach,"
and "Matilda."
    ISBN 1-57572-693-9 (lib. bdg.)
    1. Dahl, Roald--Biography--Juvenile literature. 2. Authors,
English--20th century--Biography--Juvenile literature.
3. Children's stories--Authorship--Juvenile literature. [1. Dahl,
Roald. 2. Authors, English.] I. Title. II. Series.
PR6054.A35Z77   1998
823'.914--dc21
   [B]   98-23293
                                        CIP
                                        AC

Acknowledgments
The Publishers would like to thank the following for permission to reproduce photographs: Aviation Picture Library p. 11; British Newspaper Library p. 17; Buckinghamshire County Museum p. 47; Camera Press: C. Sykes pp. 25, 41; H. Tappe p. 45; Disney p. 19; Ronald Grant Archive pp. 22, 26, 30 (top), 33, 48; Chris Honeywell pp. 20, 23, 27, 30 (bottom), 31 (both) 34, 38; Image Bank: A. Becker p. 8; The Lancet p. 29; Popperfoto pp. 15, 18; Repton School p. 7; John Searle p. 5; Topham Picture Point pp. 36, 39.

Cover photograph reproduced with permission of Richard Open, Camera Press

Our thanks to Sarah Middleton for her comments in the preparation of this book.
Every effort has been made to contact copyright holders of any material reproduced in this book. Any omissions will be rectified in subsequent printings if notice is given to the Publisher.

Any words appearing in the text in bold, **like this,** are explained in the Glossary.

This is an unauthorized biography. The subject has not sponsored or endorsed this book.

Contents

Who was Roald Dahl? 4

A Boy in Wales and England 6

Working in Oil 8

Crash Landing 10

War Hero 12

Off Again: to the United States 14

"Did You Know You Were a Writer?" 16

Hollywood, Here I Come! 18

Life After Wartime 20

My Wife the Movie Star 22

Becoming a Father 24

Back to Children's Stories 26

Disaster Strikes 28

More Disaster 30

Still More Disaster 32

"An Uneconomic Diversion" 34

The Writer's Routine 36

Making Movies 38

Living Legend 40

Child Power 42

A Controversial Character 44

The Storyteller Dies 46

Was Roald Dahl
   a Good Children's Writer? 48

Roald Dahl: Timeline 52

Glossary 54

More Books to Read 55

Index 56

WHO WAS ROALD DAHL?

I n 1985 the **publicity department** at Penguin Books in London received a 5,000 word article praising the author Roald Dahl. It described his exciting early life as a war hero, his happy home in Buckinghamshire, England which he shared with his children and wife, and the way that he wrote his books in a special writing hut in his backyard.

The article said that Dahl was an exceptionally warm and friendly man, who spent "half his life performing dotty and unusual acts and going out of his way to make someone happy." But he still found enough time to write the books that had made him, without a doubt, the most popular of all living children's authors.

The person who wrote the article was clearly a big fan of Roald Dahl. And who was that person? None other than Roald Dahl himself!

A CHILDREN'S MAN

Most of what Dahl wrote was true, especially about his success as an author of children's stories. In Britain alone, from 1980 to 1990, his publishers sold 11,326,700 of his paperbacks, which was far more than the total number of children born in Britain during the same period.

Roald Dahl shares a story with his fans.

THE CRITICS SPEAK

By the time he died in 1990, young readers all over the world adored him. To them he seemed less like a grown-up author than a big child himself. He spoke their language, shared their sense of humor, and was always on their side. For the same reasons, many adults, especially **critics** and librarians, were critical of him. They said that Dahl appealed to the worst side of children in his books: to cruelty, greed, and love of rudeness. As a result, despite his huge success, Dahl sometimes felt unappreciated, which might help to explain some of his boasting. People today still argue about the true value of his work.

A Boy in Wales and England

In a children's biography of Dahl, Chris Powling wrote, "There are very few authors whose life is as fascinating as their books. It's important that you keep this in mind because Roald Dahl was one of the exceptions."

Dahl's fascinating life began on September 13, 1916. His parents were both Norwegian, but they had settled at Llandaff, near Cardiff in Wales. His father, Harald, was a rich **ship broker**, who died when Dahl was only three years old. Dahl's loving mother, Sofie, was for many years the most important person in his life. He also had an older sister, Alfhild, and two younger ones, Else and Asta, who all stayed close to him throughout their childhood and long after.

School days

Dahl went to school in Cardiff until he was nine; then he was sent to St. Peter's boarding school at Weston-super-Mare in England for four years. That was not a very exciting time for him, and things did not improve much at his next school, Repton, in the English midlands.

Dahl was tall and good at games, especially squash and boxing, but he did not seem very bright. His summer term report card of 1930 said, "I have never met a boy who so persistently writes the exact opposite of what he means. He seems incapable of marshalling his thoughts on paper."

AFTER SCHOOL

On leaving Repton at the age of 17, Dahl spent the summer in Newfoundland with the British Public Schools' Exploring Expedition. Among other challenges, the boys had to do exploring of an unmapped region in the island's center. Dahl loved being abroad and decided to look for a job that might lead to more foreign travel.

Dahl at Repton school, aged 17. One of his fondest memories of school was testing new chocolate bars for a local manufacturer.

WORKING IN OIL

In September 1934, at age 18, Dahl joined the Shell Oil Company. It had offices all over the world, and Dahl hoped that he would be sent to work in one. But first he had to learn all about the oil business, mainly in London.

He enjoyed his trainee job and got along well with the staff. Every day after lunch he would eat a chocolate bar, using the tinfoil wrapper to make a bigger and bigger ball, which he kept on his desk.

Mount Kilianjaro in Tanzania—one of the most exotic sights on his first posting abroad

Longing for more

On weekends he would take office friends to his new home in Bexley, Kent, where he now lived with his mother and sisters. One of his interests at this time was photography. He turned a bedroom at Bexley into a darkroom for developing his films. Life in England was good, but still he longed for travel and adventure.

Into Africa

In autumn 1938, Dahl was finally sent abroad—to Dar-es-Salaam, in the African country that is now called Tanzania. Along with two other young Englishmen, his job was to supply businesses over a very wide area with oil for their machinery.

Years later he wrote: "It was a fantastic life. The heat was intense, but who cared? Our dress was khaki shorts, an open shirt, and **topee** on the head. I learned to speak Swahili. I drove upcountry visiting diamond mines, **sisal** plantations, gold mines, and all the rest of it. There were giraffes, elephants, zebras, lions, and antelopes all over the place."

Even so, within a year Dahl was getting bored. On many evenings, he wrote to his mother, there was "nothing at all to do except sweat."

CRASH LANDING

Dahl's boredom ended in September 1939. That was when World War II broke out. Dahl heard that the **Royal Air Force (R.A.F.)** was recruiting men to fight for Britain. He joined as soon as he could. He was thrilled to find out that the **R.A.F.** would teach him to fly for free, whereas in peacetime the necessary lessons would have cost him about $1,600.

"Lofty" takes to the air

Since he was so tall, Dahl's fellow trainees called him "Lofty." He had to cram himself into the cockpit of his fighter plane, but he hugely enjoyed his training, flying first over the Kenyan Highlands, then in the desert of Iraq. Finally in mid–September 1940, he was ordered to join 80 Squadron for action, in western Egypt near the border with Libya.

Dahl had been given the wrong position for 80 Squadron. He flew over the area, but he could not find the spot where he was supposed to land. Then his plane's fuel began to run out. He tried to land, hit a boulder, the plane caught fire, and Dahl rolled out of the cockpit.

Wounded

"Things were beginning to hurt," he later wrote. "My face hurt most. There was something wrong with my face. Something had happened to it. Slowly I put up a

**A Tiger Moth
biplane in which
Dahl learned
how to fly
before going to
war in a Gloster
Gladiator**

hand to feel it. It was sticky. My nose didn't seem to be there… ."

He had been very badly wounded. Luckily some British soldiers were patrolling nearby. They picked him up and rushed him to a hospital in Alexandria in Egypt.

Almost two months passed before Dahl could even get out of bed. His nose had to be rebuilt, and for the rest of his life, he suffered from the damage done to his spine. He also had terrible headaches. But none of this could hold him back. After several months, when he had recovered, he flew out to 80 Squadron, which was now in Greece, to find that he had become a war hero.

War Hero

Bravery in Greece

The situation in Greece was chaotic. The British army there was in full retreat after the German invasion. According to the official R.A.F. history, "our fighters were only able to perform their task by continually taking to the air in aircraft riddled with bullets." One of these **intrepid** fighters was Lofty Dahl. His squadron leader later said, "There is no doubt in my mind that Lofty was a very good fighter pilot and very gallant."

Action in the Middle East

After Greece, Dahl was sent to another grim theater of war: the Middle East, where the **R.A.F.** was about to assist in the invasion of Syria. Again he was in the thick of the action, and by the summer of 1941, he had shot down at least five enemy aircraft. But then his injuries from the earlier crash caught up with him. He was having such bad headaches and blackouts that he was told, for his own safety, to stop flying. So back home he went to his family.

Dahl had been away from England for three years. Much had changed. As he expected, his family had left Bexley to escape the German **air raids**. But it took him awhile to find them because they had moved to another house while he was returning by sea. Eventually he tracked them down to a pretty cottage in the village of Grendon Underwood, ten miles north of Aylesbury in Buckinghamshire.

In *Going Solo*, Roald Dahl describes his feelings on returning to his family in 1942. 'I caught sight of my mother when the bus was still a hundred yards away. She was standing patiently outside the gate of the cottage waiting for the bus to come along, and for all I know she had been standing there when the earlier bus had gone by an hour or two before. But what is one hour or even three hours when you have been waiting for three years.'

OFF AGAIN: THE UNITED STATES

AT LOOSE ENDS

It was wonderful to be reunited with his mother and sisters. But what was Flight Lieutenant Dahl to do with himself now? The war was still raging and, despite his poor health, he still wanted to serve his country. In 1942 an interesting opportunity came up.

JOINING THE BRITISH EMBASSY

The United States did not come into the war until late in 1941. The British then wanted the Americans to get involved as deeply and as quickly as possible. Who better to help urge them on than a glamorous 25-year-old fighter-pilot who loved to talk about his thrilling exploits?

The Secretary of State for Air sent Dahl to the British Embassy in Washington, D.C., with the title of Assistant Air Attaché. As a **diplomat** in Washington, he became friends with many rich and famous Americans—but it was an English citizen living there who was about to change Dahl's life forever.

Dahl worked at the
British Embassy in
Washington, D.C.

"Did You Know You Were a Writer?"

A story to tell

The English author C. S. Forester was world famous for his swashbuckling sea stories about Captain Horatio Hornblower. Dahl was a great fan, so he was very excited when Forester came to the British Embassy in January 1942 especially to see him. Forester wanted to hear all about Dahl's life as a fighter pilot. Then he planned to write an account of it for American readers. Over lunch, Dahl began to give some details. But after a while, they agreed that it might be better if he wrote his story down; then Forester could rewrite it in whatever way he chose.

Putting it on paper

That night, Dahl wrote a short story, "Shot Down Over Libya." It was based on his own experiences, but he added some fictional bits to make it even more exciting. He sent it to Forester, and two weeks later he got this reply.

"Dear RD, You were meant to give me notes, not a finished story. I'm bowled over. Your piece is marvelous. It is the work of a gifted writer. I didn't touch a word of it. I sent it at once under your name to my **agent**, Harold Matson, asking him to offer it to the *Saturday Evening Post* with my personal recommendation. You will be happy to hear that the *Post* accepted it immediately and have paid one

Roald Dahl's first ever story appeared in the *Saturday Evening Post* in 1942.

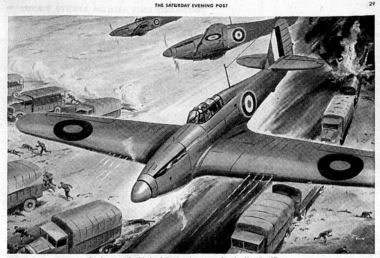

THE SATURDAY EVENING POST 29

The place was stiff with lorries of all sorts, and as we came down I could see the soldiers running about all over the place. I saw one stumble and pick himself up and go on running.

Shot Down Over Libya

"One of our planes is missing, but the pilot is safe," the communiqué said. Here is that pilot's report.

The author of this factual report on Libyan air fighting is an RAF pilot at present in this country for medical reasons—THE EDITORS.

THEY hung a label around my neck which said: "Flying Officer ——. Possible fractured skull base. Concussion and facial injuries. Church of England." I knew this because the medical orderly read the label out loud to me at the base hospital.

I tried to remember just why that label was there, and why it said these things. I tried to ask someone, but no one heard, so I gave it up and just lay still. Then slowly it all came back; not clearly and brightly at first, but a little dimly, as though by moonlight. In the end, I got it all.

Operational Order No. —— from Fighter H. Q. Western Desert to No. —— Squadron STOP Recco reports large number Italian vehicles parked close together 100 yards north of road 41 miles west of Sidi Barrani STOP Six Hurricanes attack at dusk.

The C.O. wandered in with it in his hand while we were having late tea in the mess tent, and handed it to Shorty, who was in charge of B Flight.

There was nothing unusual about the order—we had had similar ones every day for the last month—

except, perhaps, that the job looked a little easier than most.

Shorty carefully extracted a fly from his tea and flicked it across the room. Then he read it a second time. "Hell's bells, what a piece of cake! Shall I take my flight, sir? We'll have to start right away."

He handed it to Oofy, who stopped picking the sand out of his starboard ear, read it slowly, then put it down and went on excavating his ear.

"I don't believe it," he said. "They never park them close together, but if they have, what a piece of cake!"

Outside, the Hurricanes were waiting, looking very dirty in their desert camouflage, which was just a coat of light-brown paint the color of sand. At a distance they merged into their surroundings. They looked a little thin and underfed, but very elegant.

Under the wings of each, in the shade, sat a fitter and rigger playing naughts and crosses in the hot sand, waiting to help start up.

"All clear." I pressed the button; she coughed once or twice, as though clearing the sand from her throat, and started. Check the oxygen, check the petrol, brakes off, taxi into position behind Shorty, adjust tail trimmer; and now Shorty's holding his thumb up in the air. Yes, O.K., O.K. Thumb up, and everyone else does the same.

Six dusty left arms went out, six throttles were gently pushed forward and the six machines moved away, churning up the dust with their airscrews and creating a minor sandstorm in their wake. Six people began to concentrate.

Shorty swung a bit to the right on take-off, but he always did that, and we all knew he always did it, so it didn't matter. Once air-borne, undercart up, adjust the revs, regulate the mixture and start looking.

This business of looking is the most important part of a fighter-pilot's job. You've got to have a rubber neck and you've got to keep it moving the whole time from the moment you get into the air to the moment you arrive back at your base. If you don't, you won't last long. You turn slowly from the extreme left to the extreme right, glancing at your instruments as you go past; and then, looking up high, you turn back again from right to left to start all over again.

Don't start gazing into your cockpit, or, sure as eggs, you'll get jumped sooner or later; and don't start daydreaming or looking at the beautiful scenery—there's no future in it.

And so we, too, started looking. We were flying straight into the sun, which was just beginning to touch the horizon. It looked like a blood orange. Shorty was leading, with two of us close in on either side in v formation, with Oofy weaving about in the rear, watching our tails. I was on the starboard side, next to Shorty, and his wing tip was only about twelve feet away. *(Continued on Page 34)*

ILLUSTRATED BY JOHN F. GOULD

---

thousand dollars. Mr Matson's **commission** is ten percent. I enclose his check for $900. It's all yours. As you will see from Mr. Matson's letter, which I enclose, the *Post* is asking if you will write more stories for them. I do hope you will. Did you know you were a writer? With my very best wishes and congratulations, C. S. Forester."

And that was how Roald Dahl's career as a writer began.

Hollywood, Here I Come!

"Shot Down Over Libya," which Dahl later re-wrote as "A Piece of Cake," was a war story for adult readers. So were most of the other tales he wrote before the war ended in 1945. Each one was full of energy and was told in simple, dramatic language. American newspapers and magazines were eager to publish them, and they paid him well too.

Luck

Dahl could hardly believe his luck. Writers often have to work for years and years before they see their words in print. But in 1942, he had another, even bigger, stroke of good fortune. He had written the first **draft** of a story for children, and sent it, like everything else he wrote, to the British Information Services in New York. They were used to receiving material from him in his role as an official at the Embassy. But this story they sent directly to Mr. Walt Disney, who read it, liked it, and decided to make a film of it!

The great American filmmaker Walt Disney (1901–1966)

THE GREMLINS

Dahl's first children's story was about gremlins. These were originally little make-believe creatures that **R.A.F.** pilots blamed for anything that went wrong with their airplanes. Dahl developed this idea in his wacky story. He gave the gremlins girlfriends called Fifinellas and children called Widgets.

Roald Dahl's first published book was called *The Gremlins*.

He went out to Hollywood to help to prepare for the making of the film. By April 1943, over $50,000 had been spent on it but, like many war-time projects, it finally failed to reach the screen.

Dahl was not too disappointed. At least his story was published, in the United States, Australia, and Britain. *Walt Disney: The Gremlins (A Royal Air Force Story by Flight Lieutenant Roald Dahl)* came out in 1943. It was his first book.

LIFE AFTER WARTIME

After the Upheavals of war, Dahl chose to live in the quiet Buckinghamshire, England countryside to write.

In 1945, at the age of 29, Dahl went home to England. His job finished when the war ended. His mother and sisters all had houses in Buckinghamshire, and for the next six years Dahl lived with them. He chose not to go back to his prewar job with Shell Oil. Instead he aimed to make his living as a writer. This was easier said than done, even though he was already a published author.

A DIP IN FORTUNE

In 1946 most of his war stories were collected into a book titled *Over To You*. In the United States, one reviewer, Michael Straight of the *Saturday Review of Literature*, called Dahl "an author of great promise." In Britain the *Times Literary Supplement* praised the stories' "combination of ease in the telling and of **cumulative** suspense."

Dahl followed this up in 1948 with a novel for adults, *Sometime Never*, a fantasy about nuclear war. It was not a success with either reviewers or book buyers. Although the BBC had paid to broadcast some of his early stories on the radio, it was less interested in some of his newer tales, which could be quite dark and terrifying.

BACK IN THE UNITED STATES

But Dahl was still getting stories published in American magazines. He felt more appreciated in the U.S.A. than at home. Since he had plenty of friends there, in 1951 he decided to go back for awhile.

Dahl was better liked and respected in the United States than in England. To many Americans, he seemed larger than life, a born entertainer. They were prepared to put up with his boasting because he was usually such good company.

MY WIFE THE MOVIE STAR

Patricia Neal
starred with Gary
Cooper in the
1949 movie, *The
Fountainhead.*

Dahl had always had plenty of girlfriends, but when he returned to the United States he met the woman he would marry. The precise time and date of their meeting was 6:45 P.M. on October 20, 1952 at a New York dinner party given by Lillian Hellman, a well-known American playwright. For years afterward, Dahl kept that page from his pocket diary in a frame at their home. The woman's name was Patricia Neal, a talented and beautiful actress who was already on the road to stardom.

"PATRICIA NEAL'S HUSBAND"

Dahl married Pat Neal in July 1953. After a honeymoon tour of Europe, he took her home to meet his family. There was talk that one day the couple might buy a house near the other Dahls so that they could spend the summer months in England.

A CELEBRITY COUPLE

Back in the United States, they were greatly admired as a celebrity pair. Dahl's short stories for adults had been appearing regularly in U.S. magazines. In autumn 1953, a new book of his stories was published. *Someone Like You* became a runaway success and was soon translated into a number of foreign languages. Dahl loved doing promotional appearances and interviews for the book, and he was very good at them. It also did him no harm that as Patricia Neal's husband he won many new readers!

Someone Like You includes the story *Lamb to the Slaughter* about a perfect murder. A woman kills her husband by hitting him on the head with a frozen leg of lamb. The police are suspicious of her and policemen come to search the house for a murder weapon. Meanwhile the wife cooks the meat. When the search proves unsuccessful, she offers the policemen supper and gratefully they tuck into … leg of lamb

These covers show the British editions of Dahl's first collections of stories.

BECOMING A FATHER

Dahl had always been very close to his mother and sisters. Now he and Neal were eager to start a family of their own. Their careers kept them both very busy, but by the summer of 1954 Pat was pregnant. By then, as planned, they had bought a house in Great Missenden, Buckinghamshire. Sitting on five acres of land full of fruit trees, Gipsy House made a perfect writer's retreat. For years to come, Dahl and his wife would commute between here and the United States to keep to their hectic schedules.

BABY, BABY, BABY

Dahl's first child, Olivia, was born in New York in 1955. Two years later, a second daughter, Tessa, was born in Oxford, England. Then in 1960, the Dahls had a son, Theo. Dahl was a devoted father, delighting in the company of his children and closely involved in raising them.

In his 1975 book *Danny, The Champion of the World*, Dahl wrote to the reader in his typically chatty way: "You will learn as you get older, just as I learned that autumn, that no father is perfect. Grown-ups are complicated creatures, full of quirks and secrets…. What a child wants and deserves is a parent who is SPARKY."

TELL ME A STORY

Dahl especially enjoyed making up charming stories to entertain his children. These tales were somewhat different from the ones he wrote for adults. Another adult collection, *Kiss Kiss*, had been published in 1955. The book sold well, but some reviewers found the stories too gruesome, even sick. Dahl was also finding it harder to think up ideas for his stories. This worried him because he had no interest in producing fine writing for its own sake. To Dahl, the plot, preferably with a twist in its tail, was everything. So what was he going to do if his ideas for plots dried up?

Gipsy House in Great Missenden, Buckinghamshire, was the growing Dahls' family house.

BACK TO CHILDREN'S STORIES

"Roald Dahl," said Brough Girling, who had known the author in the 1950s, "had the mind of a slightly naughty eleven-year-old genius." It is hard to know if that is a compliment or not. Tastes in reading change as much as in everything else. By the mid–1950s, some adult readers were also finding Roald Dahl, the Writer, clever but rather childish. He seemed to be trying too hard to be shocking or disgusting.

CLASSIC OR CLUNKER?

Dahl was still finding it no easier to think up new plots for stories, even though his publishers wanted more. Finally, he wrote down one of the stories that he had been telling to his children and sent it in. It was titled *James and the Giant Peach*.

The picture below shows a scene from the 199? film version of *James and the Giant Peach*.

Alfred Knopf, Dahl's American publisher, liked it and published it late in 1961. There were some good and some bad reviews for this lively tale of an orphan boy who escapes on a magical peach from two cruel aunts, then travels inside it with a group of giant insects to the United States, where "every one of them became rich and successful."

CRITICS DISAGREE

One reviewer compared it favorably with *Alice in Wonderland* and said "it should become a classic." Another complained that "the violent exaggeration of language and almost grotesque characterizations **impair** the storytelling.... Not recommended."

Dahl would have to get used to such different reactions to his work for children. Meanwhile he consoled himself with the book's good sales.

Quentin Blake's illustration shows a dangerous episode in James and the Giant Peach,

One of Roald Dahl's great strengths consisted of not dressing his language up when he wrote for adults and not scaling it down when he wrote for children.
Chris Powling, *Roald Dahl: A Biography*, 1994

Disaster Strikes

Dahl's son Theo was four months old when he almost lost his life.

His nanny was pushing his baby carriage across a street in New York. A taxicab hit the pram, throwing it into the side of a bus, and crushing baby Theo. His skull was broken in many places, and even after operations he was left with hydrocephalus, or water on the brain. The American doctors felt sure he would die. But that was before his father leaped into action.

Rising to the occasion

Dr. Ed Goodman remembered, "Any new problem aroused this wonderful curiosity he had, as well as deep feeling… He kept things moving.
Roald always did that. Nothing was ever stagnant with him. He wanted to find out if there was anything to be done and to do it or to try to get someone to get at it."

Dahl, the inventor

Dahl, determined to save Theo, took him to England for treatment with specialists. There he teamed up with Kenneth Till, a **neurosurgeon** at Great Ormond Street Children's Hospital in London, and Stanley Wade, an engineer. Together they invented the Wade–Dahl–Till (WDT) valve: a gadget that could be planted in the brain to drain away fluid.

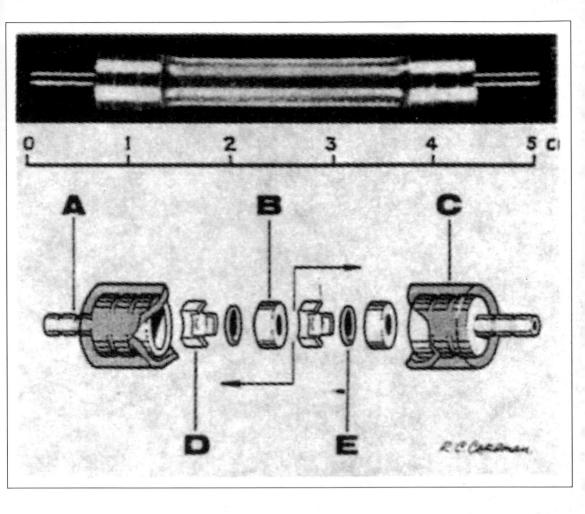

This diagram of the Wade-Dahl-Till valve was published in the medical journal The Lancet in 1964. Slowly but surely, Theo responded to his treatment. And long after he recovered, the WDT valve was used to treat up to 3,000 children with the same problem. As adults, some of them still have a valve planted in their heads today.

More Disaster

The Dahl's pose with their son Theo, after he recovered from his terrible illness.

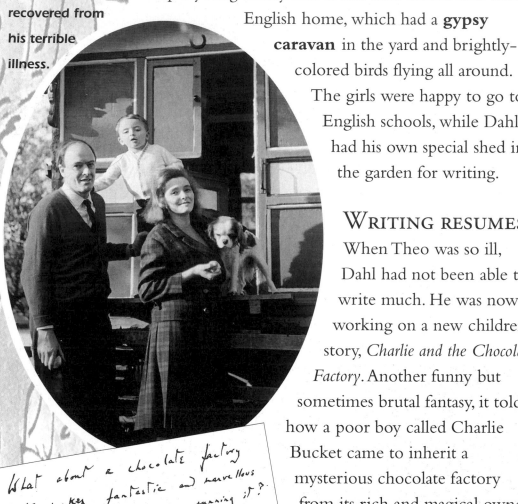

After the busy streets of New York, Great Missenden seemed a much safer place to bring up a young family. The Dahls now settled into their English home, which had a **gypsy caravan** in the yard and brightly-colored birds flying all around. The girls were happy to go to English schools, while Dahl had his own special shed in the garden for writing.

Writing resumes

When Theo was so ill, Dahl had not been able to write much. He was now working on a new children's story, *Charlie and the Chocolate Factory*. Another funny but sometimes brutal fantasy, it told how a poor boy called Charlie Bucket came to inherit a mysterious chocolate factory from its rich and magical owner, Mr. Willy Wonka.

What about a chocolate factory
That makes fantastic and marvellous
Things — with a crazy man running it?

This became *Charlie and the Chocolate Factory*.

A story about Mr. Fox who has a whole network of underground Tunnels leading To all The shops in The village. At night, he goes up Through The floorboards and helps himself.

Fantastic Mr Fox.

Dahl made these notes for possible future stories.

Olivia Dahl's grave in little Miseenden, Buckinghamshire, England and (below) a memorials to her in the local church

But suddenly in the fall of 1962, writing was the last thing on Dahl's mind. In his own words, "I feel right now as though I'll never in my life do any more." An even worse disaster than Theo's had struck the family: Olivia had died.

A FAMILY IN MOURNING

The Dahls' older daughter had caught measles. Usually measles is a mild disease, but complications set in. The seven-year-old girl went into a coma and never woke up. Neal said later that Dahl almost went out of his mind with grief. She at least managed to work afterward. She even won an **Oscar** for her performance in a movie called *Hud*. But Dahl, a practical man of nearly 50 who found it hard to talk about his feelings, seemed for a while to lose the will to live.

STILL MORE DISASTER

The Dahls battled on through their grief, and in May 1964, there was some happiness when Neal gave birth to another daughter, Ophelia. Within six months, she was pregnant yet again. Then in February 1965, the whole family flew out to Hollywood, where Neal—the main breadwinner now—was to star in a new movie.

One evening, completely without warning, she suffered three **aneurysms** followed by massive internal bleeding. After an all-night brain operation, her life was saved—but only that. Dahl took her back to Gipsy House with double vision, a literally useless right arm and leg, and an inability to read, count, talk properly, or even to remember her own children's names.

To the rescue again

In August 1965, Neal had her baby, Lucy, without problems. A year later she was walking and talking again. By 1967 she was making a new movie. It was a miraculous recovery, and due in no small part to her husband's tireless care. "Unless I was prepared to have a bad-tempered, desperately unhappy nitwit in the house," he later recalled, "some very drastic action would have to be taken at once."

A NEW THERAPY

So he devised his own form of therapy for Neal, organizing all kinds of games and activities to "unfreeze" her brain. Later he admitted, "I was often heavily criticized for pushing her too hard." Today the Volunteer Stroke Scheme uses much the same techniques. But there was nothing that even Dahl could do when his 82-year-old mother became ill in late 1967. She died on November 17, the 5th anniversary of Olivia's death.

Pat Neal starred in the movie *Hud* with Paul Newman.

"AN UNECONOMIC DIVERSION"

Faced by so many disasters, Dahl had had little time to devote to his writing. But in September 1964, *Charlie and the Chocolate Factory* was published in the United States. Within a month, 10,000 copies of the book had been sold. Soon afterward, in a *New York Times* article, Dahl made some interesting remarks.

MONEY MATTERS

"Five out of seven children's books published today are a cheat," he said, meaning that not enough work went into them. He boasted that he worked harder and longer at his books than any other current author for children, and this, he claimed, had a bad effect on his bank balance. "For one who is used to writing for adults only, it is an uneconomic diversion (a sideline which takes up a lot of time but does not pay well)." But in the years that followed, Dahl was to make a fortune from writing for children.

Roald Dahl
Charlie and the Chocolate Factory

This is the typically "down-to-earth" way that Dahl started his next book, *The Magic Finger*. "The farm next to ours is owned by Mr. and Mrs. Gregg. The Greggs have two children, both of them boys. Their names are Philip and William. Sometimes I go over to their farm to play with them. I am a girl and I am eight years old. Philip is also eight years old. William is three years older. He is ten. What? Oh, all right, then. He is eleven."

THE CRITICS STRIKE AGAIN

By March 1968 *Charlie* had sold 607,240 copies in the United States alone. It became a success in many other countries too, including Britain, where The *Times* reviewer called it "the funniest book I have read in years."

But not every reviewer found *Charlie*—or many of Dahl's later books—quite so enjoyable. Children loved reading his simple, rude, and lively books, but some adults wondered whether such books were good for children. In 1972 one U.S. critic called *Charlie* cheap, tasteless, ugly, cruel, and harmful. She even questioned "the goodness of the writer himself, his worth as a human being."

This was hard for Dahl to take, but there was more criticism to come.

THE WRITER'S ROUTINE

In later life, often in answer to questions from his fans, Dahl described in detail *how* he wrote his books, and also *where* he wrote them. He seemed fascinated by the process of writing. This was

Roald Dahl worked in the surroundings that suited him best as a writer.

possibly because, like many authors, he did not fully understand where the magic came from, and he lived in fear that one day it would desert him.

BEHIND THE WORKROOM DOOR

In his writing shed on the grounds of Gipsy House, Dahl would sit in a faded, wing chair, his legs in a sleeping-bag for warmth, resting his feet on a case full of logs, writing with a pencil on yellow American legal paper. Amid all the clutter around him was the tinfoil wrappers ball that he had made from chocolate wrappings when working for Shell Oil. Even as he grew older, and his health deteriorated, he never lost his sweet tooth.

INSIDE THE WRITER'S MIND

"One of the nice things about being a writer," he once said, "is that all you need is what you've got in your head and a pencil and a bit of paper." Dahl did not believe in going out and doing research for his books (even though in real life he loved to learn all about subjects like wine, orchids, and antiques). He relied on ideas coming to him, and after 1964 he turned these ideas into new best sellers like *The Magic Finger, Fantastic Mr. Fox,* and *Danny, The Champion of the World.*

MAKING MOVIES

Dahl had his first taste of filmmaking with *The Gremlins* soon after he started writing for a living. That movie was never made, but Dahl continued to work occasionally on **screenplays**. Writing for the screen is very different from writing books, as Dahl was to discover. The writer has to **collaborate** with all the other people who are making the movie, and Dahl was rarely a good team player.

Illustrator Quentin Blake created this world-famous image of Dahl's BFG.

UPS AND DOWNS

Most of his movie projects, including *Chitty Chitty Bang Bang* (1968) and a version of his own *Charlie and the Chocolate Factory* called *Willy Wonka and the Chocolate Factory* (1971), ended on a sour note. Dahl was unhappy because the filmmakers often hired other writers to change his screenplays.

The only screenplay that he really enjoyed working on was the one for the fifth James Bond film, *You Only Live Twice* (1967). It was based on a book written by Ian Fleming, an old wartime colleague of Dahl's in Washington. But whether the movies turned out successfully or not, Dahl was paid handsomely for his work.

Quentin Blake, who was Roald Dahl's illustrator since 1978.

A NEW COLLABORATOR

Although Dahl found it hard to work with others on movies—and he often had fallings-out with the **editors** in publishing houses—in 1978 he began to work closely and happily with a new illustrator for his books: Quentin Blake.

From *The Enormous Crocodile* (1978) on, Blake's funny, sketchy pictures helped to soften some of the harshness of Dahl's words. "It is Quent's pictures rather than my own written descriptions that have brought to life such characters as The BFG (Big Friendly Giant)," Dahl generously remarked.

One of the first Dahl books that Quentin Blake illustrated was *Revolting Rhymes* (1982), from which this short poem is one example:

"'Mary, Mary, quite contrary,
How does your garden grow?'
'I live with my brat in a high-rise flat (apartment) so how in the world would I know?'"

LIVING LEGEND

Du
uring the 1980s, as Dahl passed age seventy, he became a legend in his own lifetime. One new book after another achieved worldwide success, and he was recognized, even by his critics, as one of the most popular children's writers ever.

WRITING ABOUT THE WRITER

In 1983 a biography of Dahl for children was published written by Chris Powling. It was revised after Dahl's death 11 years later, when a more critical biography for adults was also published, written by Jeremy Treglown. Dahl's U.S. editor Stephen Roxburgh wrote to Dahl in 1983: "I think it would be so much better for young children to have your account, written as only you can write it, of whatever part of your life you choose to make open to them."

Dahl's two autobiographies told his own story his way.

LOOKING BACK AND FORWARD

Dahl thought this was such a good idea that he wrote not one autobiography but two. *Boy* (1984) covered his earliest years. Its **sequel**, *Going Solo* (1986), described his adventures in Africa and during the war. Dahl put all his usual energy and verve into writing them, and added a touch of fiction here and there for good measure. Both books sold in huge numbers and added to the Dahl legend.

At the same time, he was making a change in his personal life. In 1983, after thirty years of marriage, he and Pat Neal parted. She returned to the United States, while he got married again to an English interior decorator named Felicity Crosland, a long-time friend.

Dahl's second wife Felicity, working at Gipsy House.

CHILD POWER

In 1982 one of Dahl's best-loved books for children was published: *The BFG,* or "Big Friendly Giant." It tells the story of a dream-making giant and a little girl who work together to defeat a tribe of monster cannibals. The giant talks in an oddly confused way. He also drinks "downward-acting" lemonade, which makes him "whizzpop" from his bottom rather than burp. Children adored the book, and parents were not slow to buy it for them in suitably gigantic numbers.

"In 1991 Quentin Blake wrote, "No children"s author can surely have signed as many books as Roald Dahl: the line of the National Theatre would be across the foyer and down the stairs; and though it might take two hours, everyone had a word and a signature. This concern for his readers and his readiness to be available to them didn't end there. There were, for instance, replies to thousands of letters, both to children and teachers, with specially-written poems regularly renewed; and endless visits to schools and libraries."

From an Afterword to
The Vicar of Nibbleswicke, 1991

In the next year another Blake-illustrated book, *The Witches*, told how an old woman and a little boy collaborated to overthrow the forces of evil in the form of witches. The book won an important British **literary award**, the Whitbread Prize, which worked wonders for Dahl's ego. He began to speak about what he called his "child power." In an interview he said, "I suppose I could knock at the door of any house where there was a child, whether it was the United States, Britain, Holland, Germany, France, and say 'My car's run out of petrol. Could you give me a cup of tea?' And they'd know me. That does make me feel good."

His last full-length book, *Matilda* (1988), about a girl who overcomes her bullying parents and school principal, made Dahl an even bigger hero. In six months, half a million paperback copies were sold in Britain alone.

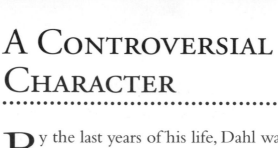

A CONTROVERSIAL CHARACTER

By the last years of his life, Dahl was a major public figure. That made him **newsworthy**. Wherever he went, people would spot him, watch him, and—usually if he was misbehaving—tell press reporters all about it. "He could be a very nasty piece of work if he wanted to," said someone who saw him take part in a local charity show, "yet he expected to be greatly admired and **deferred** to, like a very successful movie director."

STRONG OPINIONS

It is true that Dahl could be impatient, intolerant, and even vicious in his opinions, especially when his joints and back were giving him pain, or if he had been drinking. In 1979 he was thrown out of the Curzon House Club in London for making rude comments about his fellow diners. He later spoke harshly about the author Salman Rushdie, whose novel *The Satanic Verses* had provoked a **fatwa** against Rushdie from Islamic **fundamentalists**. Outbursts like these brought Dahl a great deal of bad publicity.

STRONG FEELINGS

He spoke his mind partly because he had always liked to stir people up. But he also felt that many adults, as opposed to children, did not recognize his true talents. He longed to be made a knight as a reward for his achievements as a children's writer. But he was offered only the O.B.E. (Order of the British Empire), and he turned that down. In many ways, he believed that he was always an outsider.

According to Isaiah Berlin, a famous philosopher who knew him in Washington, D.C., Dahl had no firm beliefs and was always changing his mind. "I thought he might say anything.... There was no consistent line. He was a man who followed whims, which meant he would blow up in one direction, so to speak. No doubt his imagination went into his works."
From Jeremy Treglown, *Roald Dahl*, 1994

THE STORYTELLER DIES

Dahl enjoyed his last years at Gipsy House with his second wife Felicity. His children had now grown up, but he stayed close to them all. In the summer of 1990, he threw a party for Theo's 30th birthday. Pat Neal came too, ending any bad feeling between herself and her former husband.

FINALLY A CHILDREN'S WRITER

Dahl never stopped seeing himself as a writer for young and old readers, but at the end of his life he wrote almost exclusively for children. By then, children's books were no "uneconomic diversion" for him. In Britain alone, he sold over 2 million paperback copies of his books every year.

Another collection of stories for adults had appeared in 1974, and in 1979, 31 years after his first adult novel, he published a second, *My Uncle Oswald*. Neither book was Dahl's best work. Some reviewers were very critical of them. Finally Dahl had to accept the fact that he would not be remembered as a major writer of adult fiction.

THE WORK GOES ON

Dahl need not have worried about running out of ideas for his children's books. He kept on writing until his death. *The Minpins* and *The Vicar of Nibbleswicke* were still waiting to be published when

The Roald Dahl Children's Gallery is part of the Buckinghamshire County Museum in Aylesbury, England.

he died on November 23, 1990, at age 74, after a busy promotional trip to Australia. He was buried on the hillside opposite Gipsy House. The **royalties** from all his books continue to pour in after his death. Felicity uses half of the money to help to fund the Roald Dahl Foundation. This is a charity that grants money to projects about which Dahl himself was very enthusiastic, including, quite naturally, a project teaching people how to read.

Was Roald Dahl a Good Children's Writer?

Chris Powling devoted a whole chapter to answering this question in his 1994 biography for children, *Roald Dahl*. He pointed out that children have always loved Dahl's work and that "it's only adult critics who can be so slow on the uptake," adult critics, that is, who prefer children to enjoy old–fashioned "classic" books or **politically correct** modern ones.

The 1996 film of *Matilda* starred Danny De Vito and Marci Wilson.

Powling also asked, "Could it be that Roald Dahl's books are so popular because they're the kind that children would write for each other if they had enough staying power and experience of using the language?"

Just before Dahl died, Eric Hadley remarked in *Children's Writers*, "Because he addresses his audience so directly, they have the pleasure of feeling that they are in on a tremendous joke; although this always goes with the slightly uncomfortable sense that the joke might be turned on you. This sense of sharing, of joining with Dahl in a game or plot, is crucial: you admire him and his cleverness, not his characters. He reminds me of those clever boys who haunted my childhood who were great talkers and storytellers and who told rude jokes to an admiring audience, the ones who seemed mysteriously to have more experience and who dared to *say things.*"

IS READER FRIENDLINESS ENOUGH?

Dahl, a larger–than–life character, appealed to children not just as an author but also as a person. "Roald Dahl is a man who lived through thick and thin, which is written about in *Boy* and *Going Solo*," says one nine–year–old girl in 1998. "He has written a great many books. One of my personal favorites is *Matilda*, a book about a girl that takes her time over everything, as Roald Dahl did.... I think Roald Dahl is a talented author and puts feeling into his books, which I like."

Responses like this present a problem for Dahl's adult critics. Dahl clearly succeeded in making children interested in reading, which has to be a good thing, especially in the age of TV, video, and computer games. But did he then provide children with books that were worth reading? According to the children's fiction writer Eleanor Cameron in 1972, the pleasures offered by Dahl were like those of a game show or chocolate: instantly enjoyable, but short lasting. The **feminist** Catherine Itzin made a more serious complaint when *The Witches* was published. The story, she claimed, was an example of "how boys learn to become men who hate and harm women.... Woman hatred is at the core of Dahl's writing."

MODERN CLASSICS?

Dahl started writing children's books when there were not many other reader-friendly authors around. Nowadays his conversational style and sometimes "naughty" story lines do not seem quite so unusual. It is even possible that Dahl's books made it easier for later authors, like Terry Pratchett (author of the *Discworld* novels), to get their work into print and to reach millions of readers. In future times, as newer, wilder writers come along, perhaps Dahl and Pratchett will then be seen as classic authors for children.

It is interesting to note how few books like Dahl's have been written by other authors. His style is not easy to copy, even though it is very easy to read. Dahl liked to remind people that he put a lot of effort into making his words seem to flow so effortlessly. And he always tried to have the last word in debates about the value of his work. "The job of a children's writer," he insisted, "is to try to write a book that is so exciting and fast and wonderful that the child falls in love with it." On that score at least, he was very good indeed at his job.

ROALD DAHL: TIMELINE

[First publication dates are shown for all books. (A) = Adult book]

1916	Born, Llandaff, Glamorgan
1938	Sent to Africa by Shell Oil Company
1939	Joined Royal Air Force (R.A.F.)
1940	Wounded in Western Desert
1941	Distinguished R.A.F. service in Greece and Syria
1943	*The Gremlins*
1946	*Over To You* (A)
1948	*Sometime Never: A Fable for Supermen* (A)
1953	Married Patricia Neal (divorced 1983), one son and four daughters
	Someone Like You (A)
1955	*Kiss Kiss* (A)
1961	*James and the Giant Peach*
1964	*Charlie and the Chocolate Factory*
1966	*The Magic Finger*
1970	*Fantastic Mr. Fox*
1972	*Charlie and the Great Glass Elevator*
1975	*Danny, The Champion of the World*
1977	*The Wonderful Story of Henry Sugar* and *Six More*
1978	*The Enormous Crocodile*
1979	*My Uncle Oswald* (A)

1980	*The Twits*
1981	*George's Marvellous Medicine*
1982	*The BFG; Revolting Rhymes*
1983	Married second wife, Felicity Crosland; *The Witches; Dirty Beasts*
1984	*Boy: Tales of Childhood*
1985	*The Giraffe and the Pelly and Me*
1986	*Going Solo*
1988	*Matilda*
1989	*Rhyme Stew*
1990	*Esio Trot*; Dahl died in Oxford
1991	*The Vicar of Nibbleswicke, The Minpins* published after his death.

Glossary

agent (literary) a writer's manager

air raid dropping of bombs (heavy in southern England in World War II)

aneurysm a rupture of the brain, which affects many functions of the body

collaborate work together in a joint effort

commission the agent's payment when an author's work is sold

cumulative increasing by each later addition

critic (literary) someone who reviews and evaluates books and stories

defer give in to

diplomat one who works in international relations

draft a version of a book or story (writers usually produce several)

editor person in publishing house who works with author on text

fatwa a death sentence

feminist one who advocates equal rights for women

fundamentalist (religious) holder of strictly traditional beliefs

gypsy caravan a brightly painted wooden trailer on wheels that can be lived in

impair damage

intrepid very brave

literary award annual prize given to books, such as the Booker Prize or the Whitbread prize

neurosurgeon specialist who operates on the nervous system

newsworthy information that is believed to be of public interest

Oscar award given by the Academy of Motion Picture Arts and Sciences in the United States

politically correct not causing offense to groups with special interests

publicity department department of publishing company that advertises and promotes books

Royal Air Force (R.A.F.) air force in Britain

royalty money paid to authors from the sale of their books

screenplay script for a film

sequel book or film that follows from an earlier one

ship broker agent who ships goods and insures ships

sisal plant used for making rope

topee hat or pith helmet worn in hot countries

More Books to Read

Dahl, Roald. *Boy*. New York: Viking Penguin. 1988.

Meeks, Christopher. *Roald Dahl*. Vero Beach, FL: Rourke Corporation. 1993.

Powling, Chris. *Roald Dahl*. Minneapolis, MN: The Lerner Publishing Group. 1997.

INDEX

Bexley 8, 9

BFG, The 38, 39, 42

Blake, Quentin 38, 39, 42, 43

Boy 40, 41, 49

British Embassy, Washington, D.C. 14, 15, 16

Cardiff 6, 7

Charlie and the Chocolate Factory 30, 34, 35, 38

Chitty Chitty Bang Bang 38

Crosland (Dahl), Felicity 41, 46, 47

Dahl, Harald [father] 6

Dahl, Lucy 32

Dahl, Olivia 24, 31, 33

Dahl, Ophelia 32

Dahl, Roald
    childhood 6–7
    during Second World War 10–19
    husband and father 22–5, 28, 29, 30–3, 41, 46
    in Africa 9–11
    type of man he was 4, 5, 42–5

Dahl, Sophie [mother] 6, 15, 33

Dahl, Theo 24, 28, 29, 30, 46

Danny, The Champion of the World 24, 37

Disney, Walt 18, 19

Enormous Crocodile, The 39

Fantastic Mr Fox 37

Forester, C.S. 16, 17

Gipsy House 24, 32, 37, 46, 47

Going Solo 40, 41, 49

Great Ormond Street Children's Hospital 28

Gremlins, The 19, 38

James and the Giant Peach 26, 27

Kiss Kiss 25

Magic Finger, The 35, 37

Matilda 43, 48, 49

Minpins, The 46

My Uncle Oswald 46

Neal (Dahl), Patricia 21, 22, 23, 24, 30–3, 41, 46

New York 22, 28

Over to you 21

Penguin Books 4

Powling, Chris 6, 27, 40, 48

Pratchett, Terry 50

Royal Air Force (R.A.F.) 10, 12, 19

Repton School 7

Roald Dahl Children's Gallery 47

Roald Dahl Foundation 47

Roxburgh, Stephen 40

Rushdie, Salman 44

screenplays 38, 39

Shell Oil Company 8, 20, 37

Someone Like You 23

Sometime Never 21

Till, Kenneth 28

Treglown, Jeremy 40, 45

Vicar of Nibbleswicke, The 42, 46

Volunteer Stroke Scheme 33

Wade, Stanley 28

Wade–Dahl–Till valve 28, 29

Whitbread Prize 43

Witches, The 43, 50

You Only Live Twice 39